the Country Friends® Collection

Handmade from the Heart

Kate
...stenciled 3 rooms, 17 boxes and Holly's white carpeting.

Mary Elizabeth
...made 27 seashell candles and still has enough beach souvenirs for 118 more.

Holly
...keeps repeating to herself, "It's only paint... it's only paint..."

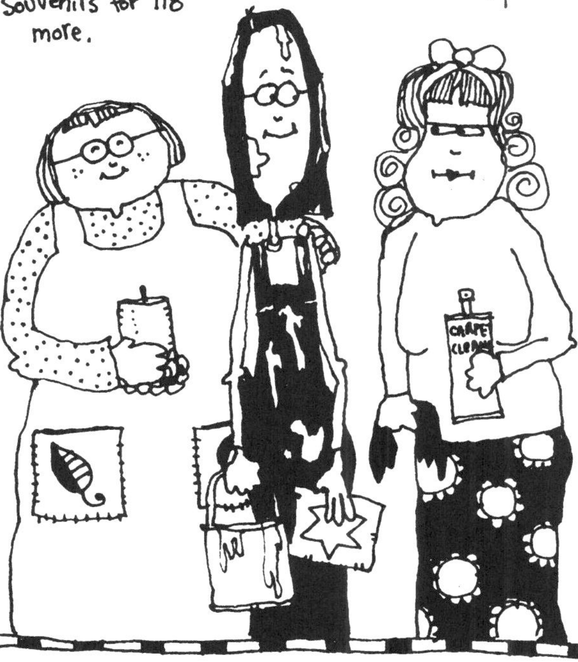

HOW TO STENCIL!

...IF THE COUNTRY FRIENDS® CAN, YOU CAN!

★

TO BEGIN, REPEAT OUR PAINT MOTTO:

Less is Best.

After loading your brush with paint, blot excess paint on to several layers of paper toweling. Too much paint will run under the stencil, making a messy design with undefined edges.

NEXT, REPEAT TO YOURSELF:

Practice makes Perfect.

Always do a test sample before working on the "real thing." It's much easier to correct mistakes and is a great way to perfect your application skills.

LOVE

WHOOPS

REMEMBER:

Patience is a Virtue.

Take your time. It is a good idea to stop what you're doing periodically to clean the paint build-up from your stencils & brushes during the stencilling process to maintain the fine details of your design. Thoroughly dry brushes & stencils before using again. Remember, too, that when using more than one color in a project, it's important to let each color dry completely before adding another.

They sure know a lot of mottos.

☆ 2

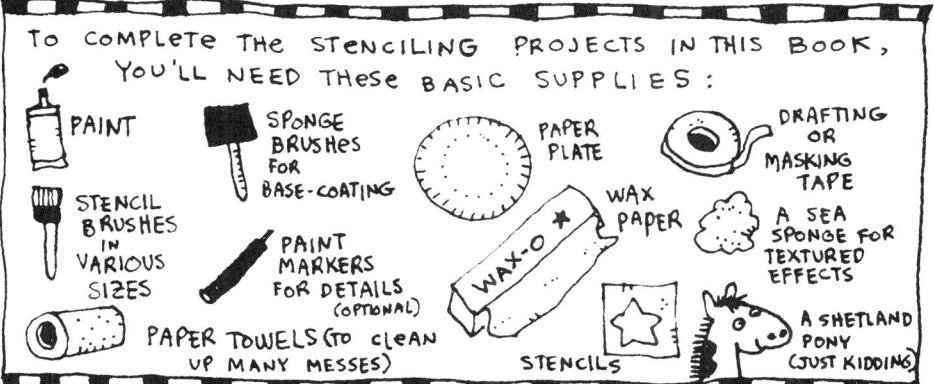

To complete the stenciling projects in this book, you'll need these basic supplies:

PAINT

SPONGE BRUSHES FOR BASE-COATING

STENCIL BRUSHES IN VARIOUS SIZES

PAINT MARKERS FOR DETAILS (OPTIONAL)

PAPER TOWELS (TO CLEAN UP MANY MESSES)

PAPER PLATE

WAX PAPER

WAX-O

STENCILS

DRAFTING OR MASKING TAPE

A SEA SPONGE FOR TEXTURED EFFECTS

A SHETLAND PONY (JUST KIDDING)

TiPs TO TrY

HOLLY'S

WHILE YOU'RE PRACTICING:

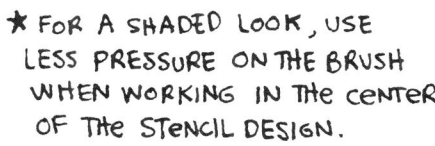

★ WORK PAINT FROM OUTSIDE EDGES TO THE CENTER IN A CIRCULAR OR DABBING MOTION.

★ FOR A SHADED LOOK, USE LESS PRESSURE ON THE BRUSH WHEN WORKING IN THE CENTER OF THE STENCIL DESIGN.

★ A PERFECT DESIGN SHOULD HAVE CRISP, WELL-DEFINED EDGES. IF YOU'RE GETTING FUZZY EDGES OR A MESSY BLOB UNDER YOUR STENCIL, WIPE YOUR BRUSH OFF AND START WITH AN ALMOST DRY BRUSH. REMEMBER, A LITTLE PAINT GOES A LONG WAY.

IT HAS LONG BEEN AN AXIOM OF MINE THAT THE **Little things** ARE INFINITELY **the most important.** — A. CONAN DOYLE

I ♥ DID IT!

I DID IT! I DID IT! LOOK! I DID IT!

TO MAKE YOUR OWN STENCILS

YOU WILL NEED:

CLEAR ACETATE (THIN PLASTIC SHEET TO CUT STENCIL FROM)
PERMANENT FINE-LINE MARKER
CRAFT OR UTILITY KNIFE
CUTTING MAT OR PIECE OF GLASS
TRACING PAPER
PENCILS
TRANSPARENT TAPE

FOR EXAMPLE: ORIGINAL DESIGN...

#1 TRACE DESIGNS ONTO TRACING PAPER.

#2. TAPE TRACING TO A FLAT DRAWING SURFACE. COVER WITH CLEAR ACETATE ⌣ TAPE CORNERS TO HOLD IN PLACE. COPY DESIGN ONTO ACETATE USING MARKER. IF YOU PLAN TO USE DIFFERENT COLORS, YOU MAY CUT SEPARATE STENCILS FOR EACH COLOR. (IT'S HELPFUL TO TRACE THE OTHER DESIGN COLORS AS BROKEN LINES ON EACH STENCIL FOR PLACEMENT PURPOSES.) USE SOLID LINES AS CUTTING LINES.

...CUT INTO 2 DIFFERENT STENCILS FOR COLOR SEPARATION:

AN ORANGE POT...

3. PLACE CLEAR ACETATE WITH DESIGN ON CUTTING SURFACE. USE KNIFE TO CUT OUT DESIGN ON SOLID LINES. CUT CAREFULLY & SLOWLY! SOMETIMES IT'S EASIER TO ROTATE OR TURN THE ACETATE AS YOU CUT RATHER THAN MOVING THE KNIFE ⌣ YOU'LL GET SMOOTHER, CLEANER-CUT DESIGNS.

...WITH RED TULIPS. GET IT?

4. USE TRANSPARENT TAPE TO MEND CUTTING MISTAKES. COVER BOTH SIDES OF ACETATE WHEN MENDING ⌣ TRIM AWAY EXCESS TAPE IN DESIGN WITH KNIFE.

SPOTTY'S PAINT COMPANY
PAINT PRIMER

- OIL-BASED PAINTS REQUIRE A LONGER DRYING TIME BUT GIVE A VERY DURABLE SURFACE.
- ACRYLIC PAINTS ARE FAST-DRYING.
- ENAMEL PAINTS ARE WEATHER RESISTANT & HAVE A GLOSSY FINISH.
- GLITTER, PEARL & METALLIC PAINTS WILL PROVIDE SHIMMERING PIZAZZ!
- PAINT CRAYONS ARE A GOOD DRIP-FREE OPTION FOR STENCILLERS

OTHER FUN STUFF TO USE
PAINTING PROJECTS with your ~

TEXTILE MEDIUM:
TURNS ACRYLIC PAINTS INTO FABRIC PAINTS FOR FABRIC PROJECTS

CRACKLE MEDIUM OR **W**EATHERED WOOD MEDIUM:
GIVES PROJECTS AN AGED LOOK

ANTIQUE MEDIUM:
ADDS A RICH OLD LOOK TO PAINTED SURFACES

TEXTURE PASTE OR GEL:
ADDS A 3-DIMENSIONAL DESIGN TO PROJECTS

5

Kate's **T**ips on **B**eing an **A**rtist: "I have noticed that real artists usually wear a beret at a jaunty angle, and some sport goatees. You might consider either accessory to improve your painting skills."

GOODIE ♥ BOXES

Little boxes are perfect for little gifts! Fill 'em with potpourri, jewelry, candy... Surprise a country friend with a personalized case for paper-clips & rubber bands .... hide a scarf in one, or even a secret message!

Our Country Friends® are sharing 3 of their favorite patterns at right; feel free to make stenciling patterns from them, or trace them and then transfer them off onto a blank box or two for a hand-painting project!

SUPPLY LIST:

- PAPIER-MÂCHÉ OR KRAFT PAPER BOXES IN VARIOUS SIZES
- PAINT • BRUSHES • STENCILS • SANDPAPER
- ANTIQVE MEDIUM • WATER-BASED VARNISH

HOW TO:

1. BASECOAT BOXES WITH 2 COATS OF DESIRED COLOR. LET DRY THOROUGHLY BETWEEN COATS. YOU MAY WANT TO PAINT THE BOX INTERIOR, TOO, FOR A MORE FINISHED LOOK.

2. DECORATE TOP & SIDES OF BOXES WITH DESIGNS. LET DRY.

3. FOR A SLIGHTLY AGED LOOK, GENTLY SAND EDGES OF LID & BOX, REMOVING SOME OF THE PAINT.

4. BRUSH ON ANTIQUE MEDIUM OVER ENTIRE BOX & LID. WIPE OFF, LEAVING A SLIGHTLY AGED LOOK. LET DRY.

5. BRUSH ON WATER-BASED VARNISH FOR A PROTECTIVE FINISH.

USE THIS
PATTERN ...

...TO MAKE THIS
BOX !

EXTRA
TIPS :

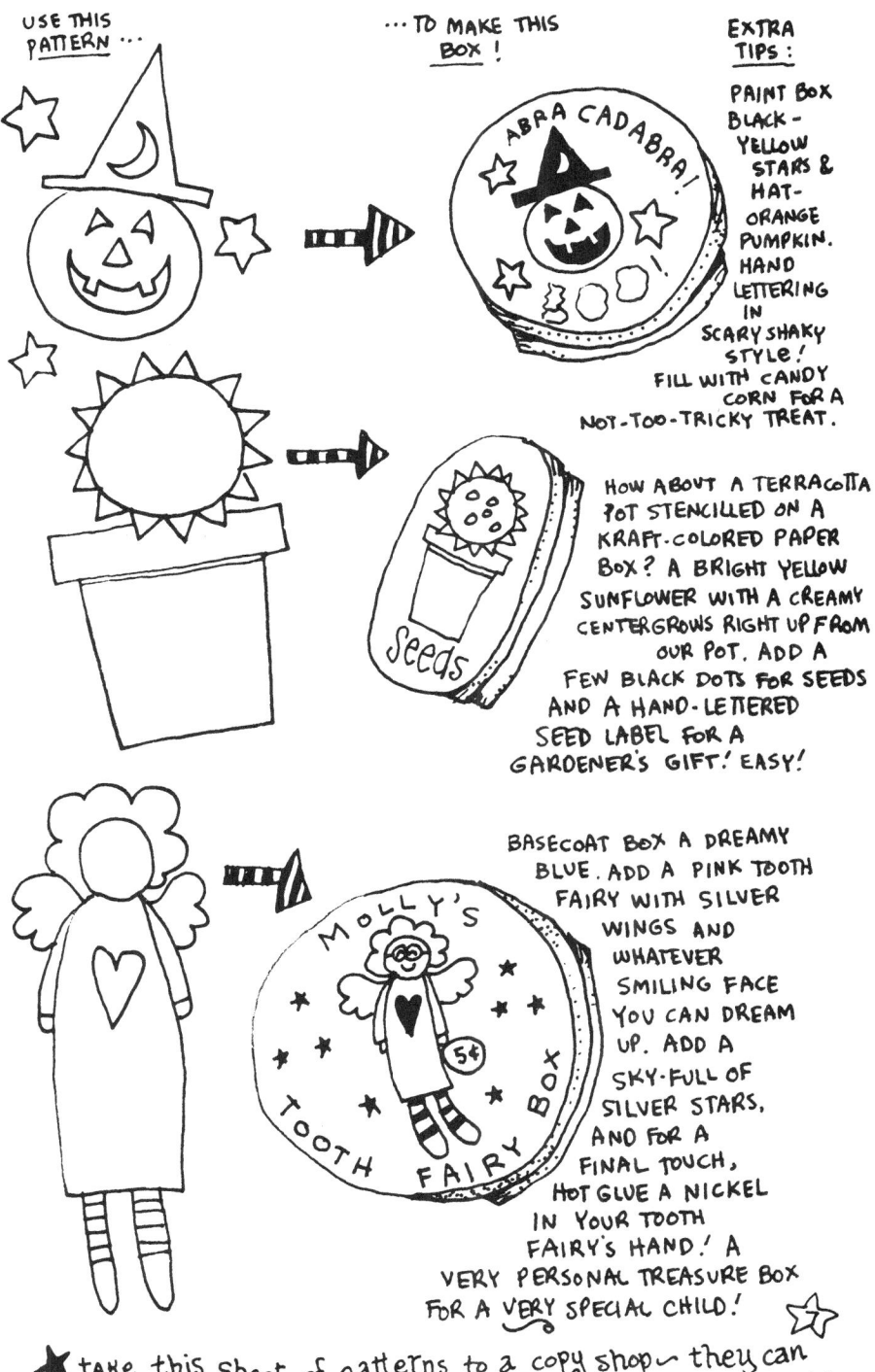

PAINT BOX
BLACK -
YELLOW
STARS &
HAT -
ORANGE
PUMPKIN.
HAND
LETTERING
IN
SCARY SHAKY
STYLE!
FILL WITH CANDY
CORN FOR A
NOT-TOO-TRICKY TREAT.

ABRA CADABRA!
BOO!

HOW ABOUT A TERRACOTTA
POT STENCILLED ON A
KRAFT-COLORED PAPER
BOX? A BRIGHT YELLOW
SUNFLOWER WITH A CREAMY
CENTER GROWS RIGHT UP FROM
OUR POT. ADD A
FEW BLACK DOTS FOR SEEDS
AND A HAND-LETTERED
SEED LABEL FOR A
GARDENER'S GIFT! EASY!

seeds

BASECOAT BOX A DREAMY
BLUE. ADD A PINK TOOTH
FAIRY WITH SILVER
WINGS AND
WHATEVER
SMILING FACE
YOU CAN DREAM
UP. ADD A
SKY-FULL OF
SILVER STARS,
AND FOR A
FINAL TOUCH,
HOT GLUE A NICKEL
IN YOUR TOOTH
FAIRY'S HAND! A
VERY PERSONAL TREASURE BOX
FOR A VERY SPECIAL CHILD!

MOLLY'S
TOOTH FAIRY BOX
5¢

★ take this sheet of patterns to a copy shop ~ they can
enlarge the designs to the size you need for your project!

PLENTY O' POTS ★ PLENTY O' POTS ★

START WITH PLENTY OF POTS 'CAUSE ONCE YOU GET STARTED, YOU WON'T WANT TO STOP!

GATHER THESE TO BEGIN YOUR PROJECT:

★

CLAY FLOWER POTS
ACRYLIC PAINTS
PAINTBRUSHES ∽ FLAT FOR BASE-COATING, FINE FOR DETAILING
WATER-BASED SEALER

A GOOD IDEA!

PAINT A MEDIUM-SIZE CLAY POT A DEEP GREEN. CUT OUT A BIG MAGAZINE PICTURE OF AN APPLE AND VARIOUS ALPHABET LETTERS. USING A DÉCOUPAGE MEDIUM (AVAILABLE AT CRAFT STORES), APPLY THE APPLE TO THE POT "BODY" AND PLACE THE ALPHABET LETTERS AROUND THE RIM OF THE POT. FINISH POT WITH SEALER. FILL THE FINISHED POT WITH LOTS OF BRIGHT YELLOW PENCILS ∽ A GREAT PENCIL-HOLDER GIFT FOR A FAVORITE TEACHER!

PLENTY O' POTS *

I THINK KATE'S MADE **TWELVE THOUSAND, FOUR HUNDRED & TWELVE**

POTS

THE BASICS:

STEP #1: PAINT THE POTS INSIDE AND OUT WITH DESIRED COLOR OF ACRYLIC PAINT. LET FIRST COAT DRY THOROUGHLY BEFORE ADDING A SECOND COAT.

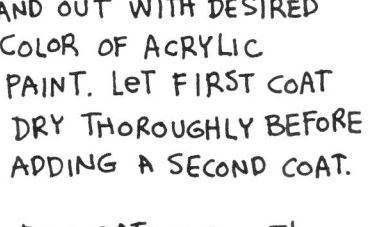

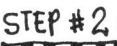

STEP #2:

DECORATE POT WITH PAINT DETAILS.

STEP #3: WHEN POT IS FINISHED, SEAL WITH WATER-BASED SEALER.

¡IDEA!

GILD A POT FOR A FANCY LOOK—

SIMPLY DRY-BRUSH METALLIC GOLD OR SILVER PAINT OVER BASE COAT, OR USE SYNTHETIC GOLD LEAF (AVAILABLE TO YOU AT MOST CRAFT STORES).

TRY A NAVY BLUE PAINT ON THE POT & JUST GILD THE RIM. *Beautiful!*

YOU MIGHT EVEN PAINT ON A FREE-HAND STAR ON THE BLUE USING METALLIC PAINT OR A GOLD PEN.

¡IDEA!

GO FOR THE *Weathered Look!*

BASECOAT POT IN A DARK COLOR. LET DRY. PAINT A LIGHTER COLOR OVER BASECOAT. LET DRY.

NOW GENTLY SCRUB POT WITH COARSE SANDPAPER OR A KITCHEN-STYLE SCRUBBER TO REMOVE SOME OF THE LIGHT-COLORED PAINT. YOU WANT TO SEE THE DARKER COLOR UNDERNEATH PEEKING OUT!

9

PLENTY O' POTS ★ PLENTY O' POTS ★ PLENTY O' POTS

USING FINE·TIP PAINTBRUSHES, APPLY LINE DETAILS AROUND POT RIMS. SQUIGGLES and DOTS are GOOD!

SPONGE WHITE PAINT ALL OVER A POT. WHEN DRY, ADD RED STRIPES AROUND RIM AND STENCIL BLUE STARS ON POT BODY. FILL WITH AMERICAN FLAGS!

HOLLY

GLUE ON A GINGHAM RIBBON FOR A QUICK DRESS-UP! JUST GET OUT YOUR HOT·GLUE GUN AND GO TO TOWN.

COOL
LOVE
U·R NEAT

PAINT A POT INSIDE & OUT WITH PINK PAINT. STENCIL WHITE & RED HEARTS ALL OVER IT. WITH A FINE·TIP PERMANENT MARKER, ADD LITTLE NOTES ON EACH HEART···JUST LIKE VALENTINE CANDY "CONVERSATION" HEARTS! THEN FILL THE POT UP WITH REAL CANDY HEARTS. FOR A SWEET Valentine pot.

BE MINE

CLAY POTS MAKE IDEAL CANDLE HOLDERS. PAINT 'EM GOLD INSIDE FOR A GLOWING SHIMMER AS THE CANDLE BURNS DOWN.

JOY

MAKE 3-D DESIGNS ON POTS WITH DIMENSIONAL PAINTS IN SQUEEZE BOTTLES.

10

A POT O' PLENTY

PAINT UP A POT FULL OF GOODIES FOR A COUNTRY FRIEND WHO HAS LATE·WINTER CABIN FEVER

PAINT A MEDIUM·SIZE CLAY POT HOWEVER YOU LIKE. (A CHEERY COAT OF BRIGHT YELLOW IS A SOUL·LIFTER!) TAKE THIS BOOK TO YOUR LOCAL COPY SHOP AND GET A DUPLICATE MADE OF THIS LABEL ⁓ YOU MIGHT ADJUST THE SIZE AS NECESSARY TO FIT THE POT. OKAY, NOW CLIP IT OUT AND APPLY IT TO THE PAINTED POT WITH A DÉCOUPAGE MEDIUM... YOU HAVE A WONDERFUL POT TO FILL WITH ALL KINDS OF GARDENING GOODIES SUCH AS:

KATE

GARDEN GLOVES (PERSONALIZE 'EM WITH FABRIC PAINT!)

ZINNIA — SEED PACKETS

A TROWEL

GOOD DIRT

SEED CATALOGS & GARDEN MAGAZINES

TULIP BULBS

COPY THIS LABEL ↘

dear country friend

· · · · · remember · · · · ·

No winter lasts forever.

Have faith ⁓ Summer is on the way!

Everything flows, nothing stays still.
— HERACLITUS

GIVE AN OLD PIECE OF FURNITURE A NEW LIFE WITH A FUN & FUNKY COAT OF

Holly's project:

AN OLD WOODEN NIGHTSTAND

FIRST THINGS FIRST ~ GET THE PIECE READY TO WORK ON! HERE ARE SOME BASIC RULES TO USE WITH AN OLD WOOD PIECE :

1. LIGHTLY SAND TO REMOVE ANY VARNISH OR LOOSE OLD PAINT. WIPE CLEAN WITH TACK CLOTH.

2. SEAL WITH WATER-BASED SEALER AND LET DRY. THIS WILL PROTECT AGAINST STAIN BLEEDING THROUGH A LIGHT COLOR BASECOAT.

3. LIGHTLY SAND AGAIN & WIPE CLEAN. YOU MAY BASECOAT IN A NEW COLOR, OR IF YOU LIKE THE RUSTIC LOOK THAT COMES FROM SANDING, GO AHEAD & START DECORATING!

Paint

SUPPLY LIST:

NIGHTSTAND
PAINT
STENCIL(S)
PAINTBRUSHES FOR
    BASECOATING,
    STENCILING & DETAILS
SPRAY STENCIL
    ADHESIVE
3/4" PAINTER'S TAPE

Here's How I Did it:
(I'M SO PROUD OF MYSELF)

1★ I APPLIED A CREAM-COLORED BASE-COAT AND LET IT DRY COMPLETELY.

2★ I CHOSE A ROSE-SHAPED STENCIL AND PRACTICED USING IT ON PAPER WITH A LIGHT PINK ACRYLIC PAINT. THEN, WHEN I WAS COMFORTABLE WITH IT, I STENCILED THE DRAWER FRONTS WITH IT, LIKE THIS :

I USED STENCIL ADHESIVE TO "STICK" THE STENCIL IN THE RIGHT SPOTS. I ALSO MARKED OFF THE AREAS NEAR THE STENCIL'S EDGES WITH PAINTER'S TAPE SO I WOULDN'T SLOP PINK PAINT WHERE IT DIDN'T BELONG!

3★ WITH A THIN BRUSH AND SOME SOFT CELERY-COLORED ACRYLIC, I DREW IN SOME VINES & LEAVES FREE-HAND.

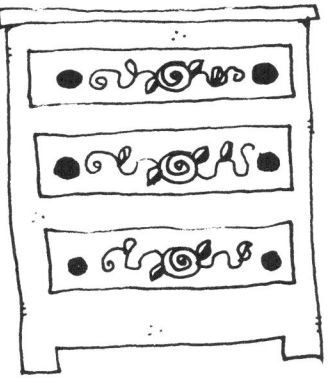

★ NOTE :
YOU SHOULD SEAL YOUR FINISHED PROJECT WITH 2 COATS OF CLEAR VARNISH.

DO YOU LOVE THAT FUN & FUNKY PAINTED FURNITURE YOU SEE IN MAGAZINES & STORES, ONLY TO BE TURNED OFF BY THEIR HUGE PRICE TAGS ?

★ HERE COME THE COUNTRY FRIENDS® TO THE RESCUE, WITH EASY DO-IT-YOURSELF INSTRUCTIONS!

HMMMM.....

Mary Elizabeth's Project:

WHAT TO DO WITH ONE

OLD CHAIR ?

SUPPLY LIST :
- WOODEN CHAIR
- DÉCOUPAGE MEDIUM
- FOAM BRUSH
- PAINT FOR ACCENTS
- VARNISH OR POLYURETHANE
- PAPER DECORATIONS (SEE LIST BELOW)

⟶ OTHER SUGGESTIONS ⟵

★1. PAINT CHAIR IF YOU WISH OR LEAVE AS IS. (I PAINTED MINE A FIRE-TRUCK RED !)

★2. FIND A BUNCH OF PAPER DECORATIONS YOU LIKE ⌣
- CUT OUT DESIGNS FROM WALL PAPER
- PHOTOCOPIED IMAGES FROM COPYRIGHT-FREE SOURCE BOOKS
- WRAPPING PAPER
- I USED MY KIDS' ARTWORK !

★3. PLAY AROUND WITH THE CUT-OUT PAPER DECORATIONS 'TIL THEY FORM A DESIGN YOU'RE HAPPY WITH. APPLY DÉCOUPAGE WITH FOAM BRUSH TO IMAGES ACCORDING TO INSTRUCTIONS ON BOTTLE. LET DRY.

★4. ADD PAINT DETAILS LIKE STRIPES, STARS, DOTS, CHECKERBOARDS ⌣ WHATEVER! FREE-HAND IT, OR USE STENCILS OR STAMPS.

★5. SEAL WITH 2 OR 3 COATS OF VARNISH OR POLYURETHANE.

COUNTRY FRIENDS®

Painted

⭐14⭐

Kate's project:

A NEW UNFINISHED STORAGE CABINET

IT NEEDS SOME PERSONALITY!
I THINK I'LL COMB-PAINT IT!

BEFORE I BEGIN, I'LL NEED TO GET IT
READY WITH THESE BASIC RULES FOR

NEW WOOD PIECES:

1. LIGHTLY SAND & WIPE CLEAN WITH A TACK CLOTH.

2. SEAL WITH A WATER-BASED SEALER. LET DRY.

3. LIGHTLY SAND & CLEAN AGAIN.

4. NOW ～ GET READY TO DECORATE!

SUPPLY LIST:

CABINET
ACRYLIC PAINT
WATER-BASED
   GLAZE IN
   NEUTRAL &
   COMPLIMENTARY
   COLOR TO ACRYLIC
   PAINT FOR
   COMBING EFFECT
PAINTER'S TAPE
PURCHASED COMBING
   TOOL
SANDPAPER
CLEAR VARNISH OR
   POLYURETHANE
(note: GLAZES &
   COMBING TOOLS
   AVAILABLE AT
   CRAFT STORES)

How To Do It:

*1. BASECOAT CABINET IN ACRYLIC PAINT.
   APPLY 2 COATS, SANDING BETWEEN COATS.
   (MAKE SURE PAINT IS DRY BETWEEN COATS.)

*2. TAPE OFF ANY AREAS YOU DON'T PLAN TO
   DECORATE TO PROTECT THEM.

*3. MIX NEUTRAL GLAZE WITH COLORED
   GLAZE. THE GLAZE COLOR SHOULD BE A
   DARKER SHADE THAN THE CUPBOARD'S
   PAINT TO ACHIEVE THE DESIRED EFFECT.
   BRUSH GLAZE ON CUPBOARD.

*4. PULL COMBING TOOL ACROSS WET
   GLAZE, CREATING A PATTERN.
   CONTINUE COMBING 'TIL YOU LIKE THE
   WAY IT LOOKS. LET DRY.

*5. SEAL WITH 2 COATS VARNISH OR
   POLYURETHANE.

Furniture

FUN & FUNKY PAINT IDEAS!

Paint dresser drawers with stripes, and the dresser's "body" with

DIP DOTS:

JUST DIP THE END OF YOUR PAINT BRUSH INTO PAINT AND TOUCH AREA THAT NEEDS A DOT!

★

GO BACK TO NATURE ~ PAINT AN OLD CHAIR A SAGE GREEN AND LEAF ~ PRINT IT IN A DARKER GREEN. SET IT OUT ON THE GARDEN PATH AND DO SOME SITTIN' AND LOOKIN'.

★

Acrylic paints work well on small projects. For larger pieces, you may want to use acrylic latex paint. (Latex paints come in economical, larger cans than craft acrylics, which come in small bottles as a general rule ~ easier on the old pocketbook!) Apply a latex primer on these projects instead of a water-based product.

★

The secret to free-handing vines is a good liner brush and thin paint. Mix paint with a drop or two of water. Load paint on brush by just touching it to edge of paint and pulling back with a rolling motion.

One
Should
Always
Aim
at
Being
Interesting
rather
than
Exact.

—VOLTAIRE

HOLLY'S no-sew PILLOWS

SUPPLIES YOU'LL NEED INCLUDE:
* FABRIC * POLYESTER FIBERFILL * AN IRON
* 3/4" WIDE PAPER-BACKED FUSIBLE WEB TAPE

1. CUT FABRIC INTO 2 SQUARES THAT ARE 1½" LARGER THAN DESIRED PILLOW SIZE.

2. DECORATE PILLOW FRONT WITH STENCILING, RUBBER STAMPS OR LEAF PRINTS. YOU CAN EVEN APPLIQUE DESIGNS USING LARGER PIECES OF PAPER-BACKED FUSIBLE WEB & DESIGNS CUT FROM FABRIC! BUTTONS OR HAND-STITCHED FELT DESIGNS LOOK GREAT, TOO.

3. ON THE RIGHT SIDE OF THE PILLOW BACK FABRIC PIECE, FUSE WEB TAPE ALONG EDGES WITH IRON. IF YOU ARE USING VERY HEAVY FABRIC, FUSE TAPE ONTO THE FRONT FABRIC PIECE AS WELL.

4. WITH RIGHT SIDES TOGETHER, FUSE FRONT & BACK PIECES TOGETHER. BE SURE TO LEAVE A 3" OPENING UNFUSED FOR TURNING & STUFFING!

5. TURN RIGHT SIDE OUT & STUFF LIGHTLY ~ DON'T PACK IT TOO TIGHTLY OR YOU'LL HAVE A "PILLOW BLOW-OUT!"

6. TURN OPENING EDGES IN AND FUSE CLOSED.

make a whole pile!

17

Holly's
Garden of Cheer

A lovely gift for a country friend with a winter birthday!

<u>YOU WILL NEED</u>:
•**FIRST OF ALL, <u>PLAN AHEAD!</u>** This particular pot needs to have a minimum of 15 weeks cold treatment in order for the bulbs to bloom. For example, bulbs planted around October 1 will bloom in January.

- Clay pot, at least 12" deep & 15" in diameter with bottom drainage hole
- stones
- potting soil
- bulbs ↪ a good mixture for this project might be:
    - 4 TULIPS - 3 DAFFODIL - 2 HYACINTH -
    - 4 CROCUS - 5 GRAPE HYACINTH
- mulch

1. Place layer of stones in bottom of pot for drainage. Top with a layer of potting soil.

2. Position tulip, daffodil & hyacinth bulbs on top of soil. Take care to leave enough space between bulbs & side of pot... bulbs can touch each other or be fairly close together. Top with 4" of potting soil.

3. Now add layer of smaller crocus & grape hyacinth bulbs. Cover with 3" of soil and about 1" of mulch.

4. Water thoroughly.

5. Expose to cold treatment (30-40°F). Place in a cool, dark place like a cellar, garage or cold frame. Check planted pot regularly— additional watering may be necessary. Do NOT LET BULBS FREEZE!

6. A good sign that bulbs are ready ↪ roots growing out of drainage hole. Bring pot indoors, water well and expose to temperatures of 40-50°F & low light for a week or so. Move to direct sunlight & night temperature of about 60°F. Keep well-watered. Give to friend with best wishes!

18

My Heart Shall be thy garden.

—ALICE MEYNELL

paper whites

forced in water

...beautiful flowers in 4-6 weeks!

YOU WILL NEED:

- PAPERWHITE BULBS
- PEBBLES
- INTERESTING CONTAINER FOR PLANTING — CLAY SAUCERS, MASON JARS, ANYTHING THAT WILL HOLD WATER

PLACE PEBBLES IN BOTTOM OF CONTAINER. PUT BULBS ON TOP OF PEBBLES. FILL IN AROUND THE BASE OF THE BULBS WITH A SMALL AMOUNT OF PEBBLES TO PROVIDE SUPPORT. ADD WATER UP TO BOTTOM OF BULBS. PLACE IN A WARM, SUNNY SPOT AND ENJOY WATCHING THEM GROW!

HOLLY'S GIFT GIVER TIP:

JUST BEFORE DELIVERING A FLOWERING GIFT, WRAP IT LOOSELY IN CELLOPHANE FOR PROTECTION FROM COLD AIR. ADD A RIBBON OR RAFFIA TO HOLD IT CLOSED.

19

COMMEMORATE A SPECIAL
DAY WITH A HAND·DECORATED
CoUNTRY FRIENDS®

Designer Plate and Mug

A SUPPLY LIST:

* PLAIN CERAMIC MUG
* CLEAR GLASS PLATE
* ACRYLIC ENAMEL GLOSS
   PAINTS IN DESIRED
   COLORS
* SMALL ROUND PAINTBRUSHES
* LINER BRUSH
* TRACING PAPER

HOW·TO:

1. WASH and DRY PLATE & MUG.

2. DECIDE ON A DESIGN — YOU WILL BE
   PAINTING ONLY ON THE OUTSIDE OF THE
   MUG AND THE BACKSIDE OF THE PLATE
   SO PAINT WILL NOT COME INTO CONTACT
   WITH ANY FOOD.

   BE CREATIVE ∼ THROW CAUTION IN
   DESIGNING TO THE WIND ∼ YOU CAN EASILY
   WIPE PAINT OFF IF YOU'RE NOT SATISFIED WITH
   THE LOOK!   ∼ OR ∼

FEEL FREE TO TRACE OUR COUNTRY FRIENDS DESIGNS —
JUST TAKE 'EM TO YOUR LOCAL COPY SHOP AND HAVE
THEM DUPLICATED IN THE CORRECT SIZE FOR YOUR WARES.
ADD DOTS, SQUIGGLES, HEARTS, STARS, WHATEVER YOU
LIKE AROUND THE BORDER OF THE PLATE, JUST FOR FUN.
(A SPECIAL MESSAGE IS A WONDERFUL WAY TO PERSONALIZE)

3. USE A PENCIL TO LIGHTLY TRACE DESIGN ON OUTSIDE OF MUG. FOR PLATE, TRACE OR DRAW DESIGN ON PAPER ⌐ TAPE TO BACK OF PLATE, THEN TRACE IT ONTO PLATE FRONT WITH A WASHABLE MARKER. REMOVE PAPER.

4. PAINT DESIGN ON MUG USING ENAMEL PAINT. ALLOW EACH COLOR TO DRY BEFORE ADDING ANOTHER. ADD OUTLINES & DETAILS LAST.

5. ON THE PLATE, DO YOUR OUTLINE & DETAILS FIRST BECAUSE YOU'RE PAINTING THE BACK OF THE PLATE. BASE COLORS ARE ADDED AFTER OUTLINE & DETAILS DRY. FOR EXAMPLE ⌐ A SNOWMAN'S NOSE, EYES & MOUTH SHOULD GO ON FIRST. THE WHITE SNOWY FACE GOES ON <u>AFTER</u> THE FEATURES.

6. FOLLOW PAINT MANUFACTURER'S DIRECTIONS FOR CURING PAINT & WASHING INSTRUCTIONS.

I'LL BE BACK AGAIN SOMEDAY!

21

SOME DESIGN IDEAS TO COPY:

FUN FOR A BIRTHDAY PLATE!

FOR A SNOWMAN FANATIC

A COOKIE PLATE FOR SANTA

FOR YOUR NEXT TEA PARTY

KATE'S ★SPICY CANNED★ ★CANDLES★

TUCK ONE OR TWO IN A GIFT BASKET!

you will need:

- ★ CLEAN, EMPTY CANS ~ CHOOSE PRETTY ONES!
- ★ PARAFFIN WAX
- ★ STIFF CANDLE WICKING
- ★ METAL WICK SUSTAINER
- ★ PENCIL
- ★ CINNAMON SCENT FOR CANDLES

★NOTE:

SAFETY WARNING: THE SIDES OF METAL CANS FILLED WITH MELTED WAX CAN BECOME VERY HOT! KEEP OUT OF CHILDREN'S REACH! PLACE CANDLES ON A STEADY SURFACE.

① MELT PARAFFIN IN A DOUBLE BOILER.

② PLACE A WICK SUSTAINER AT ONE END OF WICK. SET THAT END INTO BOTTOM OF CAN. WRAP THE OTHER WICK-END AROUND A PENCIL THAT IS RESTING ACROSS THE CAN'S RIM.

③ MIX IN CINNAMON SCENT TO MELTED WAX.

④ POUR MELTED WAX INTO CAN. FILL IN THE WELL THAT FORMS AROUND THE WICK WITH ADDITIONAL MELTED WAX.

☆22

🐝 Add Beeswax to your paraffin to lengthen burning time.

It is a good thing to be rich, and a good thing to be strong, but it is a better thing to be loved of many friends.

~EURIPIDES~

Holly's QUICK and EASY Lace Candles

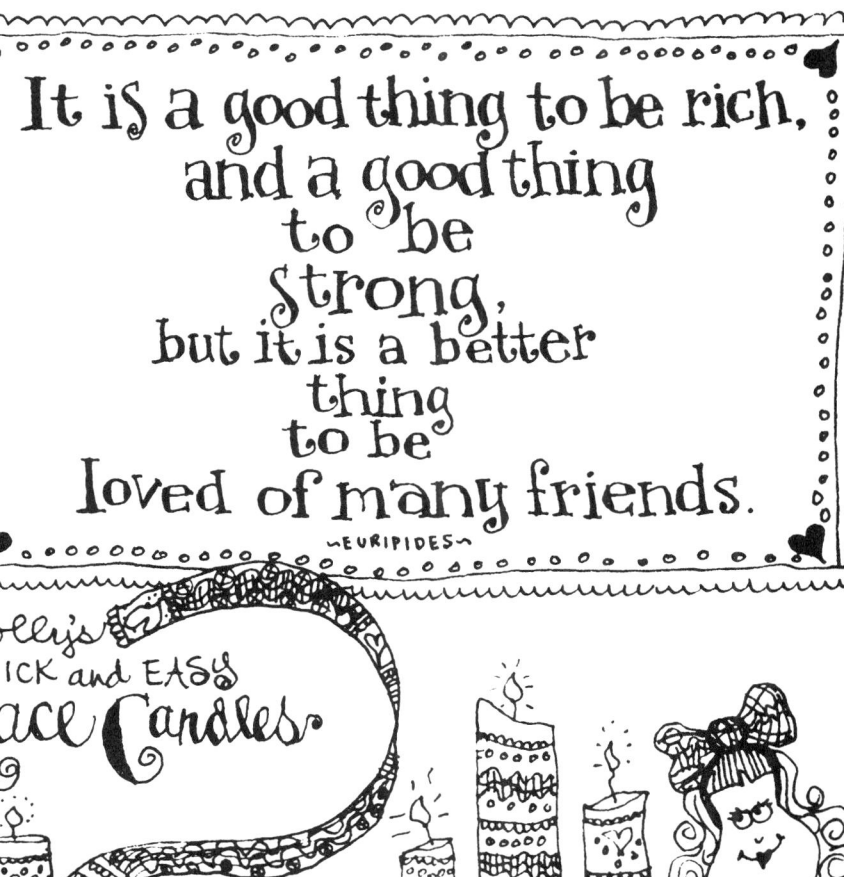

SUPPLIES
Tall pillar candles
wide lace
thin-width masking tape
metallic non-toxic acrylic
spray paints

Cut lace to fit around the candle. Place a small piece of masking tape where the two lace ends meet. (Make sure the tape doesn't interfere with the design.) Apply spray paint. Let paint dry completely before removing the lace.

ahoy!

The Shell Game

MAKE A SHELL FRAME

Add pizazz to a store-bought frame or a garage sale bargain mirror!

Simply paint your frame off-white ~ let it dry. Gently sand off the edges for a weathered look. Now ~ just glue your shells onto the frame! If you like, tuck in small bits of driftwood & Spanish moss. (Kate recommends using a quick-setting epoxy glue from the hardware store ~ it has more staying power than hot glue.)

Holly's Seashell Memory Box

Decorate the top of a wooden or papier-mâché box with small shells by just glueing them on. Let dry ~ you may want to cover your memory box with a clear epoxy coating to seal the shells to the lid.

"I like to keep my old photos from summers on the beach in my memory box — I open it up every winter and can almost feel the sand in my bathing suit."

24

Seaside Candle

a neat gift for a beach mate!

S U P P L I E S

PURCHASED PILLAR CANDLE
CLEAN, DRY SHELLS IN VARIOUS
SHAPES & SIZES
CLEAR QUICK-DRYING GLUE
OLD SAUCER OR PURCHASED
CLEAR GLASS DISH
FINE WHITE SAND

TRY TO FIND A PILLAR CANDLE
IN A MUTED SHADE OF BLUE
OR LAVENDER ⌐ A SEA COLOR.
PLACE IT ON A PIECE OF FOIL
OR WAXED PAPER.

GLUE SHELLS AROUND BASE
OF THE CANDLE WITH GLUE.
IT MAY TAKE SEVERAL LAYERS
TO FORM A RING AROUND THE
BASE. HOLLY SUGGESTS THAT
YOU START WITH LARGER,
LESS-PRETTY SHELLS FIRST AND
FINISH WITH A LAYER OF VERY
PRETTY SMALLER SHELLS. LET
DRY COMPLETELY ⌐ REMOVE
FROM FOIL.

PLACE CANDLE ON PLATE
AND SURROUND WITH A
LITTLE WHITE SAND. SCATTER
A FEW SHELLS ON THE SAND
FOR A BEAUTIFUL CENTERPIECE.

A Sand~ Bucket Full OF MEMORIES

DECOUPAGE A
FAVORITE BEACH
PHOTO ON A PLAIN
OLD PAINT BUCKET
YOU'VE SPRAYED
TURQUOISE. FILL
WITH SHELLS &
SAND, OR SHELLS
& POTPOURRI IN
A SEASIDE
SCENT!

The Hand that Gives, Gathers.

—ENGLISH PROVERB

25

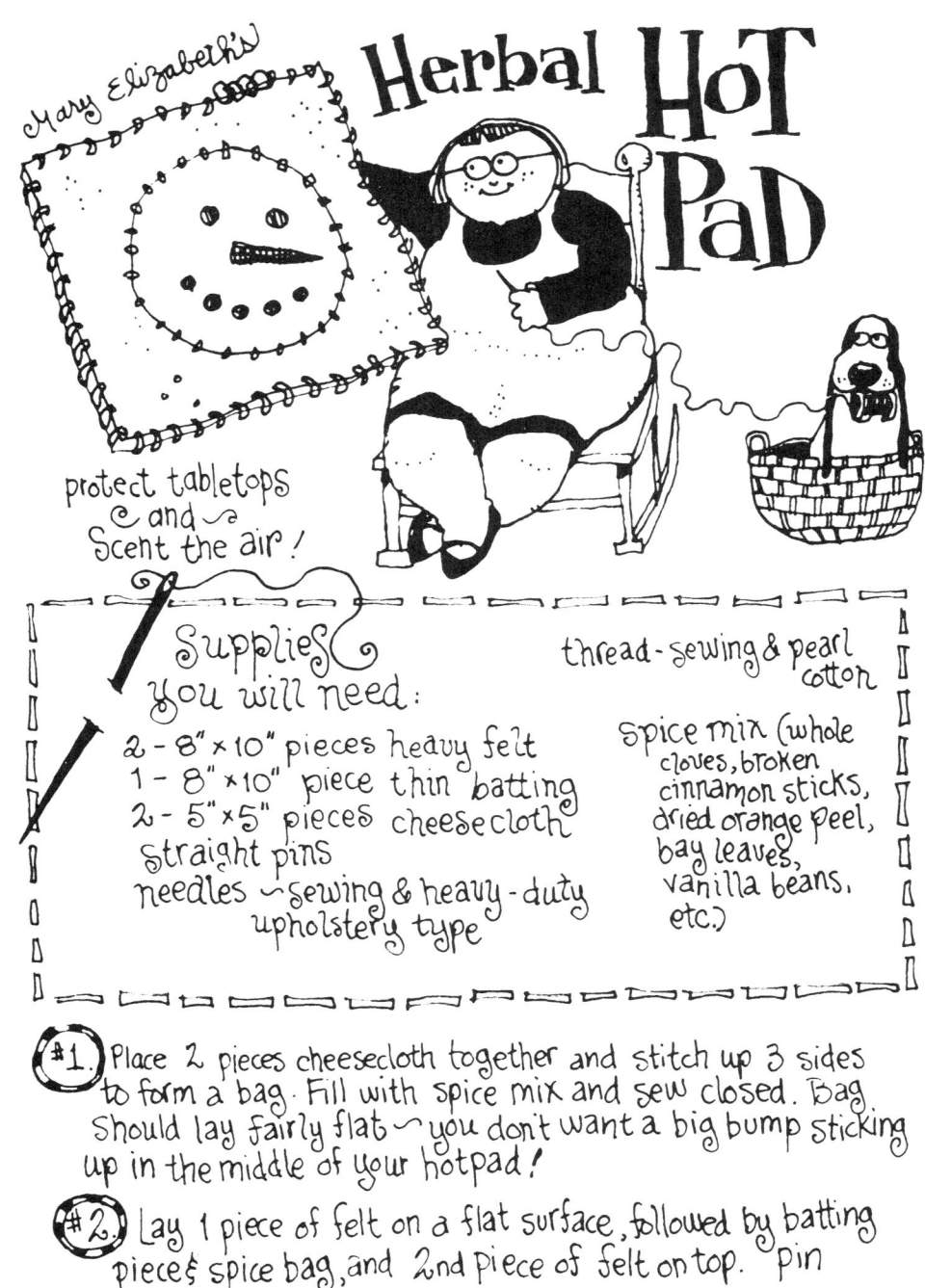

Mary Elizabeth's Herbal Hot Pad

protect tabletops
and
Scent the air!

Supplies you will need:

2 – 8" x 10" pieces heavy felt
1 – 8" x 10" piece thin batting
2 – 5" x 5" pieces cheesecloth
straight pins
needles ~ sewing & heavy-duty
upholstery type

thread - sewing & pearl cotton

spice mix (whole cloves, broken cinnamon sticks, dried orange peel, bay leaves, vanilla beans, etc.)

#1. Place 2 pieces cheesecloth together and stitch up 3 sides to form a bag. Fill with spice mix and sew closed. Bag should lay fairly flat ~ you don't want a big bump sticking up in the middle of your hotpad!

#2. Lay 1 piece of felt on a flat surface, followed by batting piece & spice bag, and 2nd piece of felt on top. Pin together.

JUST LIKE THIS
YOU GOT IT?

FELT
SPICE BAG
BATTING
FELT

#3. Stitch raw edges with pearl cotton thread using a blanket stitch.

#4. Cut primitive shapes from contrasting felt pieces and stitch by hand to top of hot pad. You can design your own or use Mary Elizabeth's idea below:

GOOD OLD SAM the COUNTRY FRIEND® SNOWMAN

I started with dark green felt for the hotpad and made Sam's face from white felt for good contrast. His eyes and mouth are simple french knots and his nose is orange thread roughly embroidered on. (If you put eyes on Sam a little crooked, or if he ends up with a missing tooth, don't fret ~ Sam doesn't care!) You can hand-wash Sam with mild soap & then air-dry him.

27

SLUMBER PARTY FUN!

KIDS WILL HAVE GREAT FUN MAKING SLEEP SHIRTS! FOR ADDED ENTERTAINMENT, DECORATE A MATCHING PILLOW CASE FOR EACH GUEST.

1 ON A LARGE COVERED AREA, LAY OUT SHIRTS & PILLOWCASES. PLACE A BIG PIECE OF CARDBOARD INSIDE THE SHIRTS & CASES SO PAINT DOESN'T BLEED THROUGH.

2 POUR A THIN LAYER OF PAINT ON TO SEVERAL PAPER PLATES. SOFTEN SPONGES IN WATER & WRING OUT COMPLETELY. GENTLY DIP INTO PAINT—BLOT EXCESS OFF ONTO PAPER TOWELS. PRESS PAINT-SPONGE ONTO SHIRT OR PILLOWCASE TO TRANSFER DESIGN. REPEAT AS DESIRED WITH DIFFERENT SPONGE SHAPES. LET DRY.

3 ADD DETAILS & DIMENSION WITH PUFF & GLITTER PAINT. (ON PILLOWCASES, YOU MIGHT ADD THE DETAILS TO THE BORDERS ONLY AS IT MIGHT BE A LITTLE SCRATCHY TO SLEEP ON.)

YOU WILL NEED:
- SPONGE SHAPES
- FABRIC PAINTS
- FABRIC MARKERS
- PUFF PAINTS OR GLITTER FABRIC PAINTS IN SQUEEZE BOTTLES
- GLOW·IN·THE·DARK PAINT
- X-LARGE PLAIN WHITE TEE SHIRTS
- PLAIN PILLOWCASES

4 AFTER PAINT IS DRY, ADD MESSAGES & NAMES WITH FABRIC MARKERS.

NOW GO TO SLEEP. (NO MORE TALKING)

ANNIE

SUSIE

Amy

molly

28

KATE'S RUSTIC STICK FRAME

A Wonderful Adirondack look ~ make a leaf print to go inside or frame your favorite outdoor photo!

SUPPLIES

PICTURE FRAME, WITH AT LEAST 1½" WIDE FLAT FRONT

BROWN ACRYLIC PAINT

TWIGS OR CINNAMON STICKS (SHOULD BE CLOSE TO SAME SIZE IN DIAMETER)

HOT GLUE OR EXTRA-THICK WHITE CRAFT GLUE

1. PAINT FRAME BROWN IF LIGHT IN COLOR. LET DRY.

2. MEASURE WIDTH OF FRAME. CUT STICKS INTO SMALL PIECES USING THAT MEASUREMENT. TRY TO MAKE THE STICKS PRETTY EQUAL IN LENGTH.

3. GLUE STICKS AROUND FRAME.

come forth into the light of things. Let nature be your teacher.

— WORDSWORTH

29

Back · to · Nature

Leaf printing

TRY THIS ON LOTS OF DIFFERENT ITEMS — PAPIER MÂCHÉ BOXES, TABLE LINENS, SHEETS & PILLOWCASES — THEN DECORATE KRAFT PAPER FOR MATCHING GIFT·WRAP!

gather these supplies:

- FRESH LEAVES SUCH AS MAPLE, OAK, ELM, IVY, PARSLEY, SAGE, MINT, VIOLET, GINGKO & SCENTED GERANIUM IN A VARIETY OF SIZES

- ACRYLIC PAINTS
- FABRIC PAINTS OR TEXTILE MEDIUM (USED WITH REGULAR ACRYLICS) FOR FABRIC PROJECTS

- GOLD GLITTER FABRIC PAINT OR PEARL PAINT

- ARTIST PAINTBRUSHES, LARGE & SMALL

LET US PERMIT NATURE TO HAVE HER WAY. SHE KNOWS HER BUSINESS BETTER THAN WE DO.
—MONTAGNE

30

How To Leaf print:

#1. WITH THE LARGE BRUSH, APPLY DESIRED TYPE OF PAINT TO THE UNDERSIDE OF THE LEAF. PLACE LEAF, PAINT SIDE DOWN, IN DESIRED SPOT.

#2. WITH FINGERTIPS, GENTLY PRESS OVER ENTIRE LEAF TO ENSURE A GOOD PRINT. VERY CAREFULLY REMOVE LEAF. USE A SMALL BRUSH TO FILL IN AREAS ON YOUR PROJECT THAT DID NOT COMPLETELY PRINT. LET DRY. YOU CAN ALSO ADD DETAILS LIKE VEINS TO YOUR PRINTS WITH GOLD OR DARKER PAINTS IF YOU WISH. AND REMEMBER-IT DOESN'T HAVE TO BE PERFECT, JUST AN INTERESTING IMPRESSION.

LEAF PRINTING Handy Hints
from the country friends®

To help flatten leaves that are a little on the curly side, try ironing leaves between 2 sheets of waxed paper with a warm iron — remember doing that in grade school? Remove leaves from waxed paper, then print with them. The fresher the leaves, the easier the job!
~HOLLY

Take your kids on an autumn nature hike and collect interesting leaves. Come home and leaf-print some tee shirts as a souvenir of your fall day in the woods. ~MARY Elizabeth

Do not, under any circumstances, leaf-print with poison oak or poison ivy.
~KATE

31

QUICK-AND-EASY JiFFY QUILT

Patch together a dolly (or doggy) quilt in a snap! A great introduction to quilting for young seamstresses....

YOU NEED:

- FABRIC SQUARES (IN COORDINATING FABRICS)
- FABRIC FOR BACK (SOLID OR PRINT)
- BIAS BINDING
- POLYESTER BATTING
- THREAD
- FLOSS
- DARNING NEEDLE

1. Sew together squares to form a patchwork fabric in the desired project size.

2. Lay materials together like so:
← PATCHWORK FABRIC
← BATTING
← BACKING FABRIC

3. Stitch all layers together around all 4 sides. Finish edges by sewing bias binding around quilt.

← BIAS BINDING

4. Sew floss ties at patch corner points, going completely through batting. Tie floss in knot; leave strings long, if you wish, or clip short. **IDEA!** Sew a bright button on each corner as you tie your floss knots!

← FLOSS TIES

Holly's Tips for filling a great GIFT·BASKET

🎀 **CHOOSE A THEME.** For instance, Mary Elizabeth loves to sew, so I filled a small sewing basket with a project book, thread, needles, embroidery floss, rolls of homespun fabric ~ all kinds of sewing goodies!

🎀 **BUILD A DISPLAY IN THE BASKET.** Put things in at varying heights ~ build a "false bottom" in the basket if need be, with tissue paper, excelsior, even styrofoam peanuts! Put tall stuff in the back of your display ~ small items in front. Tie something interesting to the basket handle ~ I added a tiny pair of scissors tied on with a homespun scrap of material. She loved it!